Teach Us to
Pray

Teach Us to Pray

TAMYRA HORST

Pacific Press®
Publishing Association

Nampa, Idaho | Oshawa, Ontario, Canada
www.pacificpress.com

Cover design by Kristin Hansen-Mellish
Cover design resources from LightStock
Inside design by Aaron Troia

Copyright © 2016 by Pacific Press® Publishing Association
Printed in the United States of America
All rights reserved

You can obtain additional copies of this book by calling toll-free 1-800-
765-6955 or by visiting http://www.adventistbookcenter.com.

Library of Congress Cataloging-in-Publication Data
Names: Horst, Tamyra, 1961- author.
Title: Teach us to pray / Tamyra Horst.
Description: Nampa: Pacific Press Publishing, 2016.
Identifiers: LCCN 2016030167 | ISBN 9780816358489 (pbk.)
Subjects: LCSH: Prayer—Christianity.
Classification: LCC BV210.3 .H655 2016 | DDC 248.3/2—dc23 LC
record available at https://lccn.loc.gov/2016030167

July 2016

Dedication

Dedicated to a God who has pursued me persistently, loved me relentlessly, and continues to teach me how to know Him more.

" Then you will *call* upon Me

and go and *pray* to Me,

and I will *listen* to you.

And you will *seek* Me and *find* Me,

when you *search* for Me

with all your *heart*."

—JEREMIAH 29:12,13

Contents

Chapter 1

First Prayers

I don't remember a time when I didn't pray. As far back as my memories go, I remember talking to God. That might not seem weird to most people, but I really don't know where I learned to pray—or why I kept praying every night. My family didn't attend church. No one prayed with me before I went to bed. My parents had gone to church growing up, but once they were married and began raising a family, they stopped. Mom blamed me—said every time the preacher stood up to speak, I began crying. So they stopped going to church. Thought they'd wait until I got a little older and could sit through the service quietly. But before that could happen, there was another crying baby. And then another. And another. By the time I was four and a half, I had four brothers. And church became an impossibility for an overwhelmed mom.

I do remember my dad praying. I can see him in my memories, even now, sitting at the head of our kitchen table with the entire family gathered around it. Once Mom had dinner on the table, we would gather and Dad would bow his head. With his hands, toughened from hard work, clasped together, he would thank God for the meal. Then everyone would start talking and passing bowls and platters of food. Our mealtimes were loud and full of conversations. A time to reconnect and talk about our day—school, work, and engines (I had four brothers, so lots of conversations centered on engines and cars and things I had no interest in).

My dad had no interest in church, so those dinner-time thank-you-for-this-meal prayers were pretty much the extent of our connection with God. Once, when I asked him if we could read the Bible, Dad gathered my two oldest brothers and his King James Bible. We sat on his bed and began to read. But it was hard to understand. Hard to read. We were just beginning to learn to read at the time, and the words and language were difficult for our elementary-school brains. We grew bored and lost interest and that was the end of that. Yet I felt drawn to God. I wanted to know more about Him.

Truly, "The Lord has appeared of old to me, saying: 'Yes, I have loved you with an everlasting love; Therefore with lovingkindness I have drawn you' " (Jeremiah 31:3).

I can still picture one summer afternoon, sitting in the back row with other neighborhood children, gathered under a tree in the front yard of my friend Susan's home. Every day for a week, a couple of teenagers with an adult mentor came and told stories. One was an exciting story from another place in the world. I don't remember many details except that they would tell the story, and just as it was getting exciting, they'd end the story for the day. To learn what happened, you had to come back the next day. Guess that's how they kept us coming back.

But there was also a second story each day—the exciting, cliff-hanging story—and a story about God. I know they told stories every day for five days, but the only thing I remember from that long-ago summer was the one thing that changed my life. God loved me. *Me.* This scrawny, way-too-shy little girl who didn't think anyone really noticed her. I wasn't the cute baby like my youngest brother, Byron. I wasn't mature beyond my years and already hardworking instead of playing (a value in our childhood home) like my brother, Nile.

I liked to cartwheel and play with dolls and had no interest in cars and engines—which made me a bit of a misfit in my all-guy family.

I was too shy and fearful to try talking to new people. I barely talked to people I knew (something hard for people who know me now to believe!).

I was the kid chosen last for recess kickball and spent most of those outdoor breaks from schoolwork swinging on the swings or climbing the monkey bars with a couple of other nonathletic kids.

I just didn't fit in or measure up to what I thought everyone else wanted. Now I was hearing that God loved me just the way I was. I didn't have to get an A in math (my least favorite subject). I didn't have to practice my clarinet (Mom and my music teacher thought I should practice for half an hour every day). God just loved me the way I was.

Could it be true? Could someone really love me for me?

I wanted it to be true. I wanted someone to love and accept me. I knew I wasn't perfect or amazing or anything special, but I wanted someone to love me anyway. To notice me. To want to talk to me and listen to me. Really hear me.

So I listened as those teenage summer missionaries invited us to accept Jesus as our Savior, to pray, and to give Him our lives. I was way too shy to go forward when they invited kids to come and pray with them. But I heard what they said and tried to remember everything. Then I ran home to my little bedroom to invite God into my heart.

I remember kneeling by my bed in that upstairs bedroom with the turquoise and pink-flowered wallpaper and praying that first prayer of commitment. I don't remember the exact words, but I did what they said. I confessed to God that I was a sinner and asked Him to forgive my sins, then I told Him that I believed that Jesus had died for me and invited Him to live in my heart forever.

As I got up off my knees, I had this assurance that I now belonged to Him forever. And if it was true that He loved me—me, this awkward, messy little girl who wasn't perfect and who felt like no one else really noticed her—then I wanted to be His girl for the rest of my life.

I didn't really know what that meant or how to live like His girl, but I began praying every day, believing that He loved me and would guide me.

What about you?

God loves you too. Just the way you are. You don't have to measure up. You don't have to get it right. He loves you and invites you to commit your life to Him. All you have to do is accept His invitation—a simple prayer, inviting Him to be your God and Savior. He won't reject you. He has already chosen you. Ephesians 1:4–6 promises, "Long before he laid down earth's foundations, he had us in mind, had settled on us as the focus of his love, to be made whole and holy by his love. Long, long ago he decided to adopt us into his family through Jesus Christ. (What pleasure he took in planning this!) He wanted us to enter into the celebration of his lavish gift-giving by the hand of his beloved Son" (The Message).

He chose you. He delights in you. He wants a relationship with you. His love will change your life—He's promised.

It starts with a simple prayer that begins a friendship that will change your life. It has mine.

Chapter 2

Connecting Prayer

I believe God smiled at my child-faith that so easily believed that He loved me and then loved Him back—even without knowing much about Him. How do you learn about God when you can't go to church and don't have someone in your life teaching you about Him?

I kept praying. Every night. I'm sure the prayers were simple. After all, I didn't really know how to pray. The only person I ever heard praying besides those teenage missionaries was my father each evening at dinner. His prayers taught me to thank God for what I had and pray for those I loved—a simple formula.

A few years later, our family moved from the suburbs to an old farmhouse with a rickety barn and one white cat that came with the place and kept us supplied with kittens. My dad quickly added a dog, then a pony, and a goat. One by one, he found animals who needed a home and brought them to live in our growing "farmette"— much to my mom's dismay. By summer, we had goats, chickens, calves, ponies, and bunnies; and we were learning to ride and take care of animals.

Despite all the animals and space to climb trees and build forts (my brothers) or sneak away to read (me), Mom found herself with a houseful of bored kids come August. So when a local church stopped by to invite us to Bible school every evening for two weeks—they'd supply transportation—she quickly said, "Yes, *please* take them!" (I'm sure she didn't say it quite like that—but I'm guessing that's what she was thinking.)

For two weeks, I learned stories about Jesus, sang songs, made crafts, and eagerly took it all in. When the church members invited us to come for church each weekend, I excitedly held my breath wanting very much for my mom to say yes again. And she did.

I was about thirteen—an age when many church-going kids start wishing they didn't have to be there. Yet here I was excited that I got to go and finally learn more about this God who loved me. I began attending church and kept up my habit of praying those simple thank-You-God-and-bless-my-family prayers each evening before bed. I loved God and wanted to do whatever He wanted me to do. I wanted to learn how to be a good Christian, pray better, and know more.

For the next several years, I tried to learn what it meant to be a good Christian. I tried hard to do the right things, say the right words, and look the part—measure up. I watched people at the church to see what Christians looked like and did. I continued to pray, trying to learn how to pray "right" by listening to other people pray. But the harder I tried to look like a good Christian, the more I felt like a failure. I was trying so hard, but I just couldn't seem to get it right.

Finally, in frustration, I cried out to God, "Lord, what do you want? What do you expect? Teach me how to know you!"

An honest, heartfelt, desperate prayer.

And God heard. He loves answering prayers like that.

"Then you will call upon Me and go and pray to Me, and I will listen to you. And you will seek Me and find Me, when you search for Me with all your heart" (Jeremiah 29:12,13).

When I finally gave up trying to look good and started looking at God, life got a lot less stressful. Instead of trying so hard to please God, I began learning how to know God. I kept praying, "God help me to really know you."

I began by reading the Bible. My dad's King James Version still seemed hard to understand, but I discovered that there were a lot of other versions of the Bible out there. I took the time to read different versions and found one that was easy for me to understand and began reading. I love stories and hadn't learned many Bible stories growing up, so that's where I began: reading stories, underlining verses that stood out to me, writing notes and prayers in the margin, and memorizing some of the Scriptures that were meaningful to me or were promises I wanted to remember.

My Bible is an important part of my journey. I eventually bought a wide-margin Bible so I had more room to write my notes and thoughts and prayers. It is like a journal of my walk with God. Today I sometimes draw pictures in the margin that not only help illustrate what I've learned, but pop out on the page when I'm skimming through, instantly reminding me of the lessons or thoughts I want to remember.

It was important to me to understand what I believed and why I believed it. At the church I was attending, people seemed to have differing beliefs about a few things. So again I prayed, "God, please show me what to believe and why to believe it."

About this time I met a man at work—a cute young man. Before long we started dating, but I noticed that we never went out on Friday evenings and I didn't see him until later on Saturdays. That seemed a little strange. So I finally asked him why, wondering if he was dating someone else on Fridays. But he wasn't. He was keeping the Sabbath. This led to a few questions. What is the Sabbath? Why didn't he just go to church on Sunday like everyone else?

He showed me from the Bible how God had set aside the seventh day as a day of rest, the Sabbath, at Creation (Genesis 2:2, 3). It was to be a day of resting from our work and connecting more deeply with God. He also showed me how God had commanded His people to remember the Sabbath (Exodus 20:8–11). He invited me to spend a Sabbath with him. I went to church with him—a church where people greeted me warmly and seemed genuinely happy to meet me. We spent the afternoon hiking. I was amazed at how many different plants and birds he knew. Afterward, he began studying the Bible with me, helping me to understand different things he believed.

Sabbath quickly became one of my favorite days of the week—a whole day to focus on God! To get together with others who believed in Him; to talk about Him and study the Bible together; to stop thinking about work and rest; to enjoy His presence; and to get outside and breathe fresh air.

That cute young man continued to study with me. God was answering my prayers. He was showing me what to believe and why to believe it. (And I really liked His choice of teachers!) I eventually chose to join his church. The church celebrated when the two of us were baptized by immersion as we publicly showed our commitment to God. (The members also seemed pretty excited when we decided to get married the following year.)

As I continued to study, I read that God gave each one of us gifts and wanted us to use them (1 Corinthians 12). I began praying that God would show me what He wanted me to do and began looking for ways to get involved at my new church. When I prayed, "God, I'll do whatever you ask me to do!" I had no idea the adventure God had in store for me or the places He'd take me. He has consistently asked me to step out of my comfort zone and do things that I didn't think I could but have ended up loving. That shy, little girl, who prayed a simple prayer of commitment and grew into a young woman who longed to serve Him and know Him but was still pretty fearful, became a woman who speaks to audiences across the United States. He didn't let me hide in the background for long but invited me to lead a ministry that required me to talk to a lot of people I didn't know. Taking each new step caused me to be completely dependent on Him. But it also taught me how to really pray—a lot of desperate, Lord, I-don't-think-I-can-do-this-without-You prayers!

I was amazed that God trusted me enough to invite me to do the things I was doing. I was amazed by the way He used me to touch the hearts of other people—in fact, I'm still amazed! Sometimes it was simply following His nudge to write a note to someone, later discovering that it came at just the right moment to encourage the person. Other times it was hearing how God had encouraged or challenged someone by something I had written or from listening to me talk.

God was showing me that He loved me, that He was with me, guiding me, teaching me, and loving people through me. I had felt like a nobody for so long, I didn't think I could ever make a difference in the world. But to God, I was somebody. And with Him, I could make a difference.

God was answering my prayers and helping me get to know Him. He was becoming not just a big God of the universe out there somewhere who loved me but a personal God who taught me and guided me each day.

What about you?

God wants you to know Him too. Prayer is one of the first places to begin. Ask Him to help you know Him better. Talk to Him just like you would a friend.

One way He speaks to us is through the Bible. Many people think the Bible is hard to read or understand. You can begin by finding a version of the Bible that is easier to read. Just go online to BibleGateway.com and pick a few verses, then read them in several different versions. Choose the version that makes the verses easy for you to understand. I often read a passage I'm studying in several different versions just to look at it from different angles.

When you begin studying the Bible, don't set goals to read a certain amount. Just begin reading and stop when something stands out to you. Think about it. Write notes. Draw a picture that reflects what you're reading. Ask God to help you understand. Bible study isn't something we "should" do, such as an item we need to accomplish and then check off. It's about getting to know God. Connecting with Him. It's more important to walk away from reading the Bible with a new understanding about God than it is to read a certain amount of text.

It's often helpful to study with someone else. Find a small-group Bible study through a local church. Ask someone to study with you one-on-one. I've often enjoyed being a part of women's book clubs, too, reading books that help us know God better. And sometimes, when I'm having a hard time really getting into Bible study, I'll pick up a book that helps me connect with God.

God has also encouraged us to get together with other believers (Hebrews 10:25). Attend church. Worship God with other believers. Combine your talents and abilities to serve Him with others, building friendships with each other, encouraging one another, and building each other up (1 Thessalonians 5:11). Together we can help each other grow, connect with God, and offer strength to face life's toughest moments.

Church can also be a great place to begin discovering ways you enjoy serving God. There are typically lots of different opportunities, but you can also serve God simply by doing what you love for others. Do you enjoy writing? Write notes of encouragement to people you know are struggling. Enjoy cooking? Make dinner for a new mom or a family battling an illness. I know a group of women who like to knit and crochet, so they get together and make lap blankets for older people who are confined to wheelchairs, praying for those who will receive their gift.

That's what it's about. Connecting with God through prayer, Bible study, Sabbath, and even by the things we do for Him. Going to church and serving Him doesn't make us better Christians. They are another way to deepen our relationship with Him.

Chapter 3

Intentional Prayer

From those first simple prayers to that desperate prayer to learn more about God, praying has been an important part of my life. Much of my prayer life has focused on praying for others. In the beginning, my list of people to pray for consisted mostly of family and friends. Every night, I would pray for these people whom I loved.

At some point, I remember praying one night for my grandmother—I always prayed for her. Trouble was, she had died months earlier. Yet here I was still praying for her without even thinking about it. That's when I realized I wasn't really praying; I was just repeating the same things over and over each night without much thought. Praying the same thing for the same people out of habit is not real conversation. I knew that needed to change. I didn't want to repeat rote words. I wanted to really talk with God. I wanted to get to know who He was and what He wanted.

So I began becoming more intentional about prayer—listening to what I was praying and not just praying on autopilot.

I learned more about how to pray by reading prayers in the Bible or verses about prayers, reading books about prayer, and by hanging out with my friend Janet. Through the Bible, God invites us to pray about everything—if it matters to us, He wants us to talk with Him about it. Janet showed me how to do that by living it out in front of me and by challenging me to pray more.

If I was worried about something or someone, Janet told me to pray about it.

If I needed to figure out what to do, she encouraged me to ask God for wisdom and guidance.

If I complained about something or someone, she challenged me to thank God.

Really? Thank God for the problems or frustrations in life? There were moments I thought she was a bit crazy and taking this prayer thing a little too seriously. Like the time I was complaining that my husband had a habit that drove me crazy. He didn't close doors. Not the closet doors in our bedroom. Not the cabinet doors in the kitchen. I was forever closing a trail of doors wherever he had been.

"Thank God for it," Janet challenged. *Really? Thank God because my husband doesn't close doors and I have to?* (I know it seems like a simple thing to be frustrated by—but I'm a very visual person and like everything neat and in its place. Janet knew that, and that's why she would make pictures crooked on the wall or move something out of "its place" whenever I left the room—to drive me crazy and see how long it would take before I fixed it. She probably loved that Tim didn't close doors!)

I remember telling God that I thought Janet was crazy, but I asked Him to help me to be grateful. A couple of weeks later when a friend's husband died, I was grateful—grateful that I had a husband who could leave doors open. It was a lesson that gave me perspective and reminded me to give thanks in all things (1 Thessalonians 5:18).

Like Janet, the Bible encourages us to pray about everything, with thanksgiving. "Be anxious for nothing, but in everything by prayer and supplication, with thanksgiving, let your requests be made known to God; and the peace of God, which surpasses all understanding, will guard your hearts and minds through Christ Jesus" (Philippians 4:6, 7). God promises that if we give Him the things we want to worry about, He'll give us peace—a peace that we can't explain.

I've experienced that peace that passes understanding. I'll never forget getting the call that my husband had been in an accident and I needed to get to the hospital right away. In the emergency room, I found my husband in a state of shock. Both of his hands and wrists were shattered from a two-story fall onto a sidewalk. Miraculously, those were his only injuries—though major. Would they be able to put his hands and wrists back together? Would he be able to use them again? Would he be able to work again? At the time, our sons were one and four, and I was a stay-at-home mom. What would we do?

As they wheeled him into surgery, I found a quiet spot and began praying. I didn't just ask God for healing, but I thanked Him that I could trust Him even in that moment. I knew God would not only get us through but I trusted that He would do big things through the accident. That's when I felt the peace surrounding me like a literal blanket. I felt this assurance that God was with me and He would take care of us.

Later that night, after my husband was out of surgery and asleep, the hospital staff told me to go home and rest. I wanted to stay there, but I was exhausted. My in-laws had our sons and had left their front door unlocked for me. After checking on my sleeping babies, I stretched out on the couch, feeling like I should still be at the hospital taking care of my husband and slowly beginning to let the fear of what we would do in the days ahead crowd my thinking. I opened my Bible and immediately read: "I will lift up my eyes to the hills— from whence comes my help? My help comes from the LORD, who made heaven and earth. He will not allow your foot to be moved; He who keeps you will not slumber. Behold, He who keeps Israel shall neither slumber nor sleep" (Psalm 121:1–4).

It was like God was telling me that it was okay for me to sleep because He didn't. He would watch over Tim—and us—all night. Again, peace filled my mind. Thanking Him for always watching over us, I was able to sleep.

Janet not only taught me to pray about everything

and to thank God but she also showed me how to pray with others—not just pray *for* other people, but to pray *with* them. That was a little scary. What if my words didn't make sense? What if I jumbled over them and didn't pray a "beautiful" prayer? Yet every time I offered to pray for someone, they seemed grateful. I learned that there's something about hearing someone else pray specifically for you—even if the prayers aren't "perfect." Praying with them ensured that I did pray. Too often I'd say I was going to pray for someone but then forget; or I'd remember a couple of times but not for long. I also began to ask God to remind me to pray for people. When I'd wake up in the middle of the night, I'd ask God to show me whom to pray for and just begin praying for people as their names popped into my head. Occasionally I'd mention to someone that I felt like God had prompted me to pray for him or her, in reply I would learn how they needed prayer—what they were going through, and how it seemed God had answered, even though they didn't know anyone was praying.

Praying for others was teaching me more about God. He really did care about people. He did answer prayer. He did speak to me. Not verbally, but by prompting my thinking—like gentle nudges.

As Janet and I continued to pray together, I listened to her prayers and realized that often, she was praying scripture verses. At first, I thought she had memorized a lot of verses, and I felt like I could never pray like that.

But then I realized that she would pray with her Bible open, often paging through to find the promises or passages that she wanted to pray and claim for someone else. She believed God's Word and prayed it right back to Him, asking Him to fulfill it in people's lives. The passages were highlighted and underlined, making them easy to find.

I began praying Scripture, too, repeating back God's Word to Him and often inserting someone's name into the verse and making it personal. My Bible has dates and names written in the margins—a reminder of when and for whom I was praying. Skimming through the pages, I am reminded of the many times I have prayed (and continue to pray) for people. As I prayed specific verses or Bible promises, they became easier to remember—I memorized them without even trying.

As I saw how prayer changed things, and people, or brought peace in tough times, I wanted to pray more. But how do you pray without ceasing when you have so many things to do? It wasn't like I could just stay on my knees all day. Not that I did all my praying on my knees. I knew that it wasn't the position of my body that made prayer powerful; it was the position of my heart and the God who heard those prayers.

So I looked for reminders to pray throughout my day. Folding laundry or cleaning the house became opportunities to pray for my family. Waking up in the middle of the night became one of the few times when I wanted to pray until falling back asleep (usually I want to stay awake when I'm praying). As I found myself worrying about something or someone, I turned those fears into prayers. In fact, I often tried to turn my thoughts into an ongoing conversation with God. It not only helped me pray intentionally but it reminded me that He was with me all the time.

Sometimes I turn the radio off in the car as I drive to work. It's a long commute, so I begin praying for my coworkers and their families—beginning at one end of the building and working my way through every office until I get through to the other side and through every floor. Or I pray for my siblings and their families—again praying for each person individually. I do this for my husband's family too. Other times I focus on my friends, praying for each of them, their concerns and struggles, and their families.

Intentionally praying, seeing God answer, and learning more about Him through prayer, has caused me to want to continue to grow my prayer life. Seeing God caring about my friends and the things—big and small—that concern me, has made Him feel close. Like the Friend He wants to be.

I love how one author describes prayer: "Prayer is the opening of the heart to God as to a friend. Not that it is necessary in order to make known to God what we are, but in order to enable us to receive Him. Prayer does not bring God down to us, but brings us up to Him."[1]

What about you?

Are you intentional about praying? Or is it a habit that you do without thinking? What is a first step you can take in becoming more intentional about turning prayer into the opening of your heart to God so that you can know Him as a friend?

You can start by praying about everything—worries, concerns, decisions, and people you love, people you're frustrated with, even people you're not sure you like at all. (You can ask God to help you see them the way He does and get a whole new perspective on them.) Remember that if it matters to you, it matters to Him because you matter to Him.

Begin thanking Him in all circumstances. You don't have to thank Him for the bad stuff, but you can thank Him that He's there and won't make you go it alone. I remember a time when a super-close friendship ended. I was devastated. I cried and cried to God yet tried to remember to be thankful. What could I thank God for in this situation? I actually asked Him, "What is there to be thankful for?" Scripture I had memorized began filling my thoughts, "I will never leave you nor forsake you;" "I have loved you with an everlasting love." I couldn't thank God that my friend had chosen to walk away from me, but I could thank Him that He never would. My friend might not like me anymore, but God would always love me. He would always believe the best about me and never give up on me.

Thanking Him didn't restore the friendship or stop it from hurting, but it did help to know I wasn't alone and that I had at least one Friend in my life who would always be there.

Intentional Prayer

As you and God begin talking more and more together, ask Him to help you pray more and to know who and what to pray for. Then follow those prompts.

Don't be afraid to pray with people. I know praying out loud scares a lot of people—we become self-conscious about our words—but God has a way of translating our prayers into something beautiful in the ears of those we're praying with. You don't have to pray long. Just pray specifically. And if you don't know what to pray, say, "God, I really don't know how to pray here, but I know You love my friend, and I ask that Your will be done."

You may want to consider inviting someone to pray with you on a regular basis—a prayer partner. You can meet over your lunch break to pray together—each sharing specific requests and the other praying for them. It doesn't have to be in person; you can pray over the phone or through e-mail too. There is something special that happens when women pray together. It can be encouraging and life changing, especially when you join forces to pray together for others. God has promised that where two or three are gathered, He's there (Matthew 18:20) and He answers prayers (verses 19, 20).

Remember that God invites us to pray. He wants us to talk to Him. Prayer is more than just praying for a list of things and people. It is a way of deepening our relationship with God.

---

1. Ellen G. White, *Steps to Christ* (Washington, DC: Review and Herald®, 1956), 93.

Chapter 4

Intercessory Prayer

While I did not regularly attend church until I was a teenager, I always recognized that God was with me. It felt like He had chosen me—like I was one of His favorites (I had never felt like anyone's favorite). As an adult looking back, I began wondering, why? Why did it feel like God was always watching out for me, protecting me, and guiding me? Putting people into my path who were key to helping me grow and take the next step in my journey with Him?

Somehow I sensed that it was because someone was praying for me—but who?

While I heard my dad pray for the meal each evening, I had never heard anyone praying for me specifically. I couldn't remember any of my grandparents ever going to church or talking about prayer. No one in my family had ever said they were praying for me.

So if prayer was making a difference in my life before I even began really praying, who had been praying for me so faithfully?

Years after my dad died, I learned that he had been

the one faithfully praying. Mom told me that throughout their entire married life, Dad never missed a night
of getting down on his knees and praying before bed.
While she never said what he prayed about—and probably didn't know—I knew. He had been praying for us.
My father loved his family more than anything else in
the world. If he was praying every night, I knew he was
praying for us.

I believe those prayers are why most of our family
now walks closely with God. My brothers and I raised
our children to know and love God. My mom committed her life to God just before my father's death. Since
then, she's been on several mission trips and volunteers
at her church and at a center near her home. At our
large (and loud) family gatherings, we continue what
Dad began and pray together before the meal. Recently
while filming my niece's wedding, my husband caught
a special moment. While I was filming the bride and
bridesmaids getting ready, he was hanging out with the
guys, catching those unscripted, before-the-wedding
moments. And when no one but my husband was
watching, those young men gathered around the groom
and prayed for him, for my niece, and for their future
together. I was surprised when I came across the footage
while editing. I don't know very many young men who
would stop and pray like that. I believe my niece has
found a godly husband partly as a result of her parents'
prayers and as a result of her own. And just this past
weekend, I listened as my brother prayed for his son,

moments before he pledged his life to his new bride. Dad would be proud to see his sons praying for and with their children.

Prayer really does make a difference. Prayer is the key to the battle each of us faces every single day. It doesn't matter if the battle is with cancer or other health concerns, with finances or work, with relationships or sin, with discouragement or insecurities. Prayer changes things. Prayer changes us. Prayer changes others. There may be moments when we feel like we can't do anything to help someone or change a situation—because it's too big or because a person just doesn't want to listen—but we can always pray. And God will change things. We just need to pray, really pray (like my dad), and intentionally commit to a time of focused conversation with God about those we love.

While I pray anytime, anywhere, my best praying happens behind closed doors. I'm focused and intentional. I'm connecting with God with no distractions or interruptions.

In the movie *War Room,* Elizabeth Jordan is a wife who discovers the power of prayer with the help of an older woman who tells her about her "war room"—the place she has set aside to pray. It's a closet she enters where she closes the door and prays—intentionally. The walls are filled with slips of papers with prayer requests she's praying about—people and situations. Elizabeth learns that there is something powerful about committing specific time to pray about specific things and people. And it changes her life, her marriage, and her family.

I've seen it in my own life, too, though I admit my commitment to prayer sometimes gets a little weak and I need to be reminded to fight with a focused intentionality. About a year ago, I was in a place where I was praying—a lot—but mostly randomly praying as I drove or thought about someone or as I was busy getting ready to go to the gym or the office. While God hears and answers those prayers, I knew that it had been a while since I had really set aside time to focus on praying and nothing else. Then God got my attention during a sermon at my church. Pastor Kris was teaching how to use the Lord's Prayer (Matthew 6:9–13) as an outline when we pray—looking at how Jesus taught His disciples to pray and using each phrase to prompt us to pray for various things including praise, confession, and intercession.

Admittedly, my mind was wandering a bit. I knew how to pray that way—had taught others how to—so I was just barely listening while skimming the other verses around this story. That's when God spoke. Not audibly, just a strong conviction that God was calling. "But when you pray, go into your room, close the door and pray to your Father, who is unseen. Then your Father, who sees what is done in secret, will reward you" (Matthew 6:6, NIV). Suddenly I felt like God was gently convicting me that I hadn't been closing the door to everything else and just hanging out with Him. I was tucking Him in around everything else I had to do. I walked away from church that morning determined to change that.

It became important to me to have a space to pray where I could actually close the door. I needed that symbolic gesture to remind me of my commitment. I chose to pray first thing in the morning before doing anything else—before checking my phone, going to the gym, heading to the office, or whatever else my day demanded—even if it meant skipping something else.

I made sure that the things I needed for this prayer time were already in the room—my Bible, my journal, and my pen. Because my mind tends to wander, I handwrite my prayers as letters to God in a journal. It's a practice I began when I became pregnant with my first son—more than thirty-one years ago. I don't worry about grammar or punctuation or spelling. I just attempt to pray honest, from-the-heart prayers. Journaling them also gives me a written record that I can go back through and see what I was praying for and be reminded of the ways that I have seen God respond and answer.

I keep Post-it® notes handy too. When I come across promises in the Bible that are meaningful to me, I sometimes write them on the Post-it® notes and put them on the wall next to where I sit. It makes it easier to remember the verses and claim them for people as I pray.

Then I spend that time praying, talking to God like a friend, honestly and simply. No big fancy words. I like to begin my time by thanking Him for specific things. I think back over the previous day and make a note of all the things I can be grateful for. I also attempt to take time to ask God to convict me of any sin. When He does, I confess it and ask Him to forgive me. He promises that He will (1 John 1:9). I ask Him to change me and help me to not give in to that sin again. I pray about things in my own life—struggles, questions, and challenges I'm facing.

But a huge part of my time is spent praying for other people. Most are people I know and love. Some are people others have asked me to pray for. I may never meet them, but I know God will hear and respond to my prayers for them. And sometimes I may not know them when I begin praying, but later God allows our paths to cross. I think He does that to encourage me and help me see what He's doing in response to my prayers. I recently connected with a young woman whose father had asked me to pray for her a couple of years ago. It's been exciting to see what God has been doing in her life even though I didn't even know the struggles she was facing.

But there hasn't been anyone I have prayed harder for than my sons. I have prayed for them since before they were born. Sometimes with tears. Sometimes angry that God wasn't answering faster and in the way I wanted. Sometimes with joy and gratitude. But always praying like crazy for them.

One of the things that has helped me the most as I've prayed for them is remembering that I don't have to convince God about anything when it comes to my sons. He loves them more than I do and wants more for them than I do. He has dreams for them that are bigger than anything I can possibly dare dream—and I am a pretty good dreamer. I remind myself of these things when I pray for them. It gives me courage and hope.

We're not invited to pray in order to change God's mind or convince Him to do something good for someone. Prayer is instead joining with God on behalf of someone else. While the enemy is out to destroy, God longs to rescue people and give them courage and hope—help them overcome bad habits, addictions, and destructive behaviors. He wants to restore relationships and heal people from pain and wounds—emotional and physical, but more importantly—spiritual. Yet God chooses to wait until invited. He has given people the power of free will. They get to choose whether to follow Him or not. Make good choices or poor. He didn't create us to be robots that perform on command, but He gives each of us the power to choose how we live. Prayer gives Him permission to move. To convict. To encourage. To protect. People still ultimately choose how they will respond to Him, but our prayers allow Him to do all He can for those we love.

What about you?

Do you believe that prayer can make a difference? Are you ready to commit to praying regularly? Who does He want you to fight for in prayer?

You don't need a "war room" to pray. You can pray in your living room or bedroom, on your porch, or while walking.

You can literally close the door or shut everything else out figuratively. You don't need to write your prayers out. You can choose to pray out loud or silently. The important thing isn't the how but discovering what will help you stay focused and committed. Then pray, believing God hears, cares, and is answering—even when He seems silent or things don't go the way you want.

Choose a time and place that works for you. Somewhere you won't be easily interrupted and distracted. While I do my best praying first thing in the morning (I'm a morning person), my friend, Jeanne chooses to pray in the evening. Pick a time that works for you.

Try a few different ways of focusing on prayer—writing or typing your prayers out, praying out loud, just jotting down the names or things you're praying for on a list. You may like the idea of a journal but don't want to write them out. You can type them into your computer or choose an online journal site.

It might be helpful to begin by creating a list with the names of those people and things you're praying for and dating it. Then when God answers, you can mark the request and thank Him for how He has moved. It's often encouraging to see a visual reminder of how many prayers God has answered—especially when we experience times when answers seem hard to find. I think that's why God often told His people to "remember," because in the tough moments, it's easy to forget that God has proved faithful in the past.

Don't forget to take time to thank God for the ways He is answering. Thankfulness changes us too. It reminds us of how God is working and builds our trust and faith.

Whatever you choose to do, just begin praying, believing that God is hearing and is responding. And when you are tempted to doubt, tell God, "I'm really struggling here. I believe, but I need you to help me really believe." God likes to answer honest prayers like that too.

Chapter 5

Battle Prayers

*If I were your enemy, I'd devalue your strength
and magnify your insecurities until they domi-
nate how you see yourself, disabling and disarm-
ing you from fighting back, from being free, from
being who God has created you to be. I'd work
hard to ensure that you never realize what God
has given you so you'll doubt the power of God
within you.*

—Priscilla Shirer, *Fervent*

As I read these words just this morning, they
rang true in my heart. It's a battle I face daily.
I can't say I fight it daily. There are days I fight—days
I recognize the voice of the enemy and his attempts to
take out my heart and keep me from being who God
created me to be. But there are way too many days when
I don't fight. When I believe the voice of the enemy
instead of the voice of my Creator. When I look in the
mirror and don't like what I see. There is a litany of

reasons why, and sometimes it occupies my thoughts way too much and keeps me distracted, discouraged, and defeated.

Can you relate?

You get up in the morning and stumble to the bathroom. The sight you see in the mirror instantly discourages you and the negative thoughts begin. *I'm too fat. Why can't I be more disciplined with what I eat? I know better. It's all my fault. Look at that hair. Why can't it ever look nice? I just colored those roots and they're already shining through! I wish I had clear, smooth skin—no freckles, no wrinkles. If only I were pretty . . .*

Your thoughts may sound a little different than mine, but I'm guessing that you beat yourself up a bit every time you look in the mirror. Oh, there may be days—moments, even—when you see your reflection and think, *Not bad.* Even times when you think you look pretty good. But if you're like me, those are few and far between—and not often enough.

You do the best you can and head out to face the day wishing you were thinner or prettier or "something-er." Something that would help people notice you and like you. Accept you. When you stop to pick up a few things at the store, the magazines near the checkouts remind you that you're not thin enough or pretty enough (all while sharing some amazing dessert that you just have to try). At work you see the woman in the next office or cubicle and feel inferior. She seems to have it all together—her looks, her clothes, her abilities. You wonder why you can't be more like her. And you instantly feel like you're not enough because you're not her. It's not intentional, but it happens all day long. That persistent measuring yourself against what you think about others.

Let's face it ladies: we tend to compare and compete without even thinking about it. We walk into a room and instantly notice every other woman—what she's wearing, her size, how attractive she is, or how many friends she has around her. We compare her outside appearance with our inside perception—how great she looks to how bad we feel about ourselves. And we end up feeling even more discouraged.

The messages follow us throughout our day. We each experience it differently, uniquely, but it boils down to the same thing: We're not enough. We will never be good enough, thin enough, pretty enough, smart enough, accomplished enough, a good enough mom, or a good enough wife. You get it. You have your own "not enough."

Then we also feel like we're too much: too messy, too faulty, too klutzy, too fat, too skinny, too silly, too loud, too talkative, too quiet, or too—you fill in the blank.

Sometimes I just want to scream! The constantness wears me out. I'm tired of feeling like I'm not enough—or too much—often both at the same time. And I wonder, "If *I* don't like me, how can anyone else? How can God like me when I'm such a mess?" It gets in the way of us praying. Of living the life God called us to. Of even believing that God has a purpose for our lives.

See, we forget one crucial piece of the story.

While we have a God who loves us (Jeremiah 31:3), delights in us (Psalm 147:10–11), will never leave us (Deuteronomy 31:6), sings over us (Zephaniah 3:17), wants to give us an abundant life (John 10:10), and gives a peace that passes understanding (Philippians 4:7) and a joy that overflows our hearts (John 15:11), we also have an enemy.

The Bible tells us that we have an enemy who is out to devour us. It compares him to a roaring lion looking for his next meal (1 Peter 5:8). This isn't some the-devil-made-me-do-it enemy. He would love for us to see him that way, as the devil tempting us to do something wrong and we just say no—or sometimes yes, but then we confess and God forgives and we just need to get our act a little more together. No, the story is much bigger than that.

The Bible compares him to a lion—a fierce hunter who is cunning and patient. He watches his prey, looks for signs of weakness, and waits for just the right moment. He quietly stalks his target. And when the moment is right, he pounces with the intent to destroy. He doesn't want to just lead the weak animal astray. He wants to destroy it and completely take it out. And the victim never sees it coming. The enemy works the same way. He studies us, looking for our weak points and watching for just the right moment, and then he pounces. He's not just trying to make us do something wrong; he wants to destroy us.

Battle Prayers

We are under attack—every single day of our lives. We just don't often live like it. We try to live good lives. Keep from sinning. And yes, the devil will tempt us to sin, but it is so much bigger than that. He wants to keep us from believing God, believing His promises, trusting Him, and serving Him. He wants to keep us from living the lives that God plans for us—abundant lives, filled with joy, peace, grace, and forgiveness. And he will do whatever it takes. It might be busyness—he'll even keep us busy doing good things when they keep us from really connecting with God. He may just try to keep us so focused on ourselves and our inadequacies that we don't have courage to really make a difference in this world. Or cause us to be trying so hard to live perfectly that we're afraid to risk and try anything new—step out of our comfort zones, because we might not be able to do it perfectly. What if we make a mistake? What if it's not the right choice? He may attempt to keep us just discouraged enough that we don't have a vision for possibilities. Discouragement is one of his most effective tools in my life. If he can get me discouraged, I lose hope and courage. It impacts every area of my life. I too easily give up and give in and feel like nothing will ever change. I will never be enough to make a difference.

He is subtle. His attacks aren't always easily recognized. Too often they feel like the truth about us. And he makes sure we hear the same messages—from a variety of sources so that it does feel like the truth. It might be the things spoken to us as kids, or heard through media—things that keep repeating over and over in our thoughts. He studies us and knows what attacks will do the most damage. His goal is always to take out our heart. To keep us from being the women that God has called us to be and playing the role He has created us to live. And he will keep making sure we hear the same messages over and over so that they become a "truth" we believe about ourselves.

One consistent area of attack in my life (there are many, but this is one I can easily share, and that I win the battle more often than not these days) is friendships. Over and over, the enemy has made sure I hear, "No one would want to be your friend."

The messages began as a kid when I couldn't rationalize the world around me and everything was about me—like it is for little children. My mom was super busy with too many babies too close together. By the time I was four and a half, I had four brothers. Mom—naturally—was overwhelmed, overworked, and tired. I'm sure it was all she could do to keep her head above water with all the babies, laundry, meals, cleaning, crying, dishes, etc. I don't know how she did it! Dad worked, sometimes two jobs, so she was doing it pretty much alone. But as a little girl, I didn't realize all of that. I just wanted my mom to pay attention to me. Play with me. Talk with me. Read to me. I couldn't understand that while she may have wanted to, it was impossible. The enemy moved in, whispering, "Your mom doesn't want to spend time with you. And if she doesn't, who else would?"

I was a shy kid. Really. Shy. So making new friends was more than hard. But I was also an observant child. I watched. Took it all in. I saw all the kids playing and laughing together from my perch on the playground swing. And I heard it again. "No one wants to be your friend."

At home, I was the only girl. My brothers paired off. Nile and Darren. Kent and Byron. Growing up, they were always with each other. Their names were automatically spoken together. They all enjoyed doing guy things. I liked dolls, cartwheels, and books. It was another subtle reminder. "You don't fit in. You don't belong. No one wants to hang out with you."

I'm sure it didn't take long for me to begin believing that it was my fault. That there was something about me that made people not want to hang out with me. And so I learned to stay busy and stay out of the way. Sadly, while I was attempting to protect my heart from rejection and hurt, I wasn't reaching out to people either. I was missing opportunities to care, connect, and encourage—things I can be good at. Others missed out on a good friendship because I wasn't willing to risk it. (The enemy often attacks the areas of our life where God can use us the most if we trust Him.)

As a young adult, I did not have a lot of friends. I typically had one or two close friends at a time. I've never been one for lots of chitchat and surface conversations, so when I make a friend, I want to connect—talk—and I tend to really care about my friends. I want to be there for them. Encourage them. Pray for them. But too many times, I saw my friendships end, for different reasons, but always with the same result. I grieved and heard again that same message: "No one really wants to be your friend. See they get to know you and discover the real you and walk away."

I remember at one point even making a decision that I would never have close friends again. It was too painful when the friendships ended. I would just do my best to encourage and care about people (I was recognizing that this was something God wanted me to do and had gifted me to do) from a distance, but I would not build friendships.

Luckily, God eventually won the battle in this area of my life. I recognized the enemy and his lies. When I'd hear that familiar rumbling, I reminded myself that it was a lie. I realized that the enemy pounded on this area of my life because he wanted to keep me from being the person God created me to be—a good encourager. Someone who likes to help people in practical ways when they're hurting and who wants to be there to listen and pray with people. When I focused on the lie, it caused me to hide who I was and kept me from seeing other people the way God wanted me to see them.

And that's the enemy's goal: to keep us from believing who God says we are and from living the life He's designed us to live. His messages are persistent and hard to identify.

What about those moments when you drop something

or trip over the crack in the sidewalk and immediately think, *You klutz! You are so not graceful!* Those words are not from God. They are the enemy—the one who accuses and emphasizes shame (Revelation 12:10). God doesn't talk that way about His daughters. And He doesn't want us to talk that way about ourselves (or others—though we are typically much harder on ourselves) either. But the enemy knows if he can keep us beating ourselves up, we won't believe that God can forgive us. Or use us to make a difference. Or believe that we have anything to offer a discussion, a person, or the world. And the worst—we won't believe that God can truly love us, because we don't really like ourselves.

First and foremost, the enemy wants to keep us from believing and trusting God. So he will attempt to keep us focused on our insecurities and inadequacies and keep us from spending time with God or trusting Him. Or believing that God really loves us—individually. *Sure He loves other people—they have it more together—but not me.* That's right where the enemy wants to keep us living.

So he tries to keep us from talking to God or studying His Word. If we did, we wouldn't lose so many battles. If we really spent time praying and studying and reminding ourselves of God's love and His promises, we would be much more prepared to fight the battle and win. So the enemy attempts to thwart any efforts on our part to connect with God.

Have you ever found yourself wanting to grow closer

to God so you make a commitment like, "I'm going to get up early every morning and spend time with God before going to work"? It might work for a couple of days, but suddenly all kinds of things begin to happen that keep you from that time. Your alarm doesn't go off. You have to go to work early. Your child gets sick and keeps you up all night. Or you get up then get side-tracked by something that needs putting away or a load of laundry that needs to be tossed in the washer, and then you see something else you forgot to do and before you know it, your time with God has slipped away and you've done everything but spend time with Him. Or, in today's cell phone age, you check your phone before checking God's Word and decide to just take a quick peek at Facebook or Instagram and soon realize you've spent the last half hour reading posts instead of Scripture. You think it's just you and get frustrated with your-self, not realizing there is an enemy who is happy that you're not hanging out with God (and that you're not recognizing his distractions or attempts to keep you from God).

He attempts to break down our friendships. Our marriages. Our relationships with our children. He would love to keep us competing with each other or feeling insecure around others—or superior to people. The devil will do anything to keep us from really being there for someone else or connecting with them or really praying for them or seeing them as someone who needs prayers and care. He doesn't want us to love one another or encourage one another in tangible ways. He likes to keep us hurting each other or feeling hurt by others or just disconnected so that we can't help each other in this journey.

The truth is we live in a love story set in a battle between God who fights for us and an enemy intent on destroying us. John writes, "The thief does not come except to steal, and to kill, and to destroy. I have come that they may have life, and that they may have it more abundantly" (John 10:10). God longs to give us hope and courage. The enemy wants to steal and destroy all God desires for us. But too often we live like there's nothing going on—it's just life. We're just trying to make it through the day, when we need to be praying fightin' prayers.

"Above all else, guard your heart, for everything you do flows from it" (Proverbs 4:23, NIV). God calls us to guard our hearts because He knows two things. First, our hearts are under attack. We have an enemy who wants us to lose heart and give up. Second, everything we do and everything we are comes from our heart.

One way I guard my heart is to begin recognizing the attack by naming the lies that fill my thinking. I remind myself of what God says and who God says I am. It's hard. The negative thoughts slip in so easily. The accusations sometimes feel so deserved and sometimes are true. I do sin. I do mess up. I am very faulty. But I also know that when God convicts me of sin, He does so gently—not to shame or accuse but to lead me to confession and repentance. He convicts of sin so that He can work in my life. Change me. Lead me deeper to Him. The enemy, on the other hand, only wants to lead me deeper into shame, guilt, discouragement, and farther from the life God has for me. So I watch for feelings of shame and guilt and discouragement and give them to God, too, asking Him to speak truth into them, confessing sin, but also asking God to take away the feelings of shame and guilt that too often paralyze me or imprison me.

There's a machete in my prayer area as a reminder that I am fighting a very real battle. It was a gift my mom brought back from one of her mission trips. I found it forgotten and tucked away in a closet. I came across it one day and decided to get it out of the back of the closet and use it—not to fight anyone but as a reminder to fight for my own heart and for those I love. I've used it as an illustration in a couple of sermons (it's amazing how much people pay attention when you're preaching with a machete in your hand!), but I really never unsheathe it or wield it otherwise. I just have it there to remind me that this is a battle. And I want to be on God's side—for others and for myself.

It's also helped me to talk with friends about the battles we each face. Most of us are fighting similar battles. Not the same specifically, but we can understand what we each are struggling with. We can encourage each other. Help each other grow stronger and more aware of the lies and God's truth. One weekend, not long ago, two friends and I were sharing a room at a women's retreat. As we went to bed Saturday night, I asked, "So what lies has the enemy been telling you today?" We had a good conversation. It surprised me—yet didn't—how my two beautiful friends; capable, intelligent women with so much to offer the world; saw themselves throughout that day—the lies they believed or had to fight against believing. Talking about it and identifying them together, we again realized that we are not alone. And the lies are not the truth about us. We encouraged each other and pointed each other to God and what He says about us.

Conversations with friends like that—real, honest caring and sharing—are incredibly helpful. But it's also important that I talk to God. I tell Him the struggles and ask Him to speak truth into my heart, to help me believe who He created me to be. To see the gifts and abilities He's given me.

It's really not about becoming more self-confident but more God-confident. Confident that He loves me. Confident that He trusts me to serve Him. Confident that He hears my prayers and responds. Confident that I am part of His story.

What about you?

As you've read this chapter, what stirred in your heart? Did you recognize yourself in some of my words? What are the areas that you struggle with about yourself? When you look in the mirror, what thoughts run through your head?

As you go through your day, how confident are you that you have a role to play that will make a difference in at least one person's life? Do you really believe that God loves you—right now, in this moment—even if you don't have it all together?

As you hear those familiar taunts throughout the day in your interactions with people—messages that often cause you to hide a little of who you are, not speak up or reach out—have you ever thought, This is the enemy trying to destroy me and keep me from living the life God has for me? *Or do you just believe that you're not enough? Do you stop to see that other person you're comparing yourself to and wonder,* What is she struggling with? How can I be a friend to her? Or pray for her?

Talk to God about it. Tell Him what you think and ask Him to help you hear His voice, to hear what He says about you, and to see other people through His eyes. Ask Him to guide you in how you can tangibly care for others—pushing past any fears or insecurities on your part. I've found that by caring for others and encouraging them in their battles, it strengthens me to fight my own.

Read your Bible, looking for what God says about you. Underline or highlight the promises in purple so they stand out. (Purple to remind you that the truth is you are a princess of the Most High King.)

What visuals would help you remember to "talk good" about yourself? You may not have a machete, but you can get a foam sword in the toy section. Or write God's promises or reminders on Post-its® and put them on your mirror, above your computer, or make them your password for your accounts so that every time you type in your password, you're reminded.

Name the lies. It can help to name it out loud and then say, "I reject this. It is not the truth about me. Devil, you have no power over me. Jesus has died for me. He loves me. He knows all about me and loves me. I am His."

Guard your heart.

God says you are worth it.

Chapter 6

Persistent Prayers

It wasn't pretty. I was hurting, upset, and angry—
at God. I had prayed and prayed and prayed for
my son, and it felt like God wasn't answering. Things
weren't getting better in his life. And nothing breaks this
mama's heart more than seeing her sons struggle and not
being able to fix it or make it better. So I prayed like
crazy. But it seemed like God wasn't listening. Or worse,
He was hearing me and not doing anything about it.

Maybe you wouldn't even call it praying. Maybe it
was more like ranting. (I am so grateful for a God who
is big enough to handle our messiness and ugliness and
still love us!) I listed for God all the things I had done
for my son throughout his life. Quit my job to be a
stay-at-home mom. Played with him. Read stories to
him. Took him to church and Sabbath School classes.
Sacrificed financially to send him to Christian schools.
Was involved at his schools throughout his education.
Prayed with him every day, often more than once.
Prayed for him constantly. Prayed for his friends. Got
to know them. We eventually changed churches so that

he could be at a place with a strong youth program. Sacrificed for him to go on a mission trip. My list was pretty long. Then begging and crying, I asked, "When are You going to do Your part, God?"

"I have loved you with an everlasting love."

I recognized that God was gently speaking to my heart. Bringing a Scripture verse I had memorized to my thoughts. But I didn't want it. I wanted answers for my son.

"I know You love me, but what about my son?"

"I have loved you with an everlasting love."

No matter what I prayed or how hard I cried, I kept hearing this verse repeated in my thoughts, as if God was softly and gently repeating it Himself.

I surrendered and turned to Jeremiah 31:3. As I read the verse, I began allowing the Scripture passage to lead me in praying for my son, turning the verses into personalized prayers and promises.

"I know You have loved my son with an everlasting love and that you draw him with lovingkindness" (verse 3).

"Build him again, rebuild his life . . . and cause him to rejoice—to have joy again" (verse 4).

"Let him want to come to you" (verse 6).

"Let him sing with gladness and praise you" (verse 7).

The ranting quieted. My heart began to become more peaceful as I prayed God's Word back to him.

"Turn his mourning to joy . . . comfort him . . . let him rejoice . . . fill his heart with abundance and let Your goodness satisfy him" (verses 13, 14).

But when I got to verse 16, I stopped dead in my tracks—er, prayers. "Refrain your voice from weeping and your eyes from tears" (I had been literally crying and crying out). "For your work shall be rewarded, says the LORD" (I had been listing all my "work"). "And they shall come back from the land of the enemy. There is hope in your future, says the LORD, That your children shall come back to their own border" (verses 16, 17).

Wow. God used verses already written—thousands of years earlier—that spoke directly and uniquely to the very thing I was praying about. I believed that God was responding to my heartfelt cries. He was encouraging me to not give up. To keep hoping. To persistently believe and pray for my son.

I definitely got up off my knees feeling more peace, joy, and courage.

Persistence can be hard. There will be moments when it feels like we have prayed and prayed and prayed and nothing has happened. There have been times when I've been frustrated that simple, silly prayers—like for a great sale price or parking space—have been answered, but the big, most important, urgent, life-impacting prayers seem to go unheard. How do you keep persistently praying? Persistently believing God cares and answers prayers when your heart is breaking and answers seem very far away?

I remember praying for my mom. For fourteen years I prayed that she would come to know God in a very real way. I remember an afternoon in my kitchen listening to a Christian radio station, and a song about God reaching those we love came on. It was a favorite song of mine. But as I sang along, the song became a prayer for my mom. I remember stopping singing and just praying and crying, "God, can you reach my mom? You're the only one who can! How long? Please, God!"

I wondered why God wasn't answering. I knew that Jesus died on the cross so that every single person—including my mom—could know God and have eternal life (John 3:16). So I knew I was praying God's will. But God sure didn't seem to be in any hurry. Why?

I prayed. I begged. I waited. Not always patiently. I never gave up because, well, where else would I turn? What else was there to do if not pray and pray? I wanted my mom to know God and believe His love for her. I wanted her to have hope and courage. I knew she was struggling—my baby brother was killed in an accident his senior year of high school. I knew she was angry with God and that she wondered if there was a God. Well-intentioned Christians, wanting to comfort my mom, told her things like, "God must have wanted him in heaven more than here." That angered my mom. She worked in a facility where elderly patients sometimes begged to die, and here God chose to let them live and instead take this vibrant young man who had a bright future and career ahead of him. "If that's the kind of God He is," she responded, "then I don't want any part of Him."

Then one spring evening, during a meeting at my church, Mom surrendered her life to God. The next week, she was baptized. It wasn't long before she was headed out on her first mission trip to Nicaragua with a group of people she didn't even know.

I don't for one minute believe that God suddenly found Himself sitting in heaven with nothing to do and said to an angel, "Hey, pull a prayer request and let's answer it." That is not how He works. I believe that God was working all along, I just hadn't seen it. Looking back, I can see some of the ways He had been moving my mom towards Him. The love she felt from members of my church as they filled my parents' dining room table with dishes of food to help feed those who joined us after my brother's funeral. And the women who befriended her when she attended church events with me. (My dad would always tell her, "Mary, they're having this thing at Tami's church. You should go. Remember what they did for us when Byron died.") I watched her slowly believe that maybe, just maybe, God could love and accept her too. God gently led her to the place of committing her life to Him. My prayers were being answered all along.

Sometimes we have our eyes so focused on seeing the end result that we miss what God is doing. It's not that He isn't answering. He is. Sometimes it just takes longer to get the "finished result" that we're looking for. But He is answering.

And sometimes the answer doesn't look like what we want it to look like. People often say that God responds yes, no, or maybe. I think that's too easy of an answer.

And I don't think it works quite like that. I think that God says *yes* every single time. But what He says *yes* to is more of Him. He gives us Himself in answer to our prayers.

I remember my friend Becky talking about how someone reprimanded her for having weak faith. Becky lives with pain and disabilities as a result of a car accident. Someone told her that if she just prayed with enough faith, God would heal her. That she just didn't have enough faith. I love her response! She told the person, "I believe that it takes more faith to live unhealed—with the pain and disabilities—than it would take to live healed." Her answer has always stayed with me because it's so true! We want the easy answers, but sometimes God just wants to give us enough strength and courage to depend on Him as we walk through it.

Even Paul the apostle prayed three times for God to remove something from him, but God said *no*. Paul shares the story in 2 Corinthians 12.

And lest I should be exalted above measure by the abundance of the revelations, a thorn in the flesh was given to me, a messenger of Satan to buffet me, lest I be exalted above measure. Concerning this thing I pleaded with the Lord three times that it might depart from me. And He said to me, "My grace is sufficient for you, for My strength is made perfect in weakness." Therefore most gladly I will rather boast in my infirmities, that the power of Christ may rest upon me. Therefore I take pleasure in infirmities, in reproaches, in needs, in persecutions, in distresses, for Christ's sake. For when I am weak, then I am strong (verses 7–10).

Like Becky, Paul recognized that sometimes when it appears God is saying *no*, He's actually offering more of Himself—His strength, His courage, His peace.

Martha and Mary learned this as well.

They were sisters and good friends of Jesus. He often visited in their home in Bethany. Their friendship grew to a place where they absolutely trusted that He loved them. So when their brother, Lazarus, was sick, they sent a messenger to tell Jesus, "The one you love is sick" (John 11:3, NIV). They didn't ask Him to come. They trusted that He loved Lazarus and would either come and heal him or just say the word and Lazarus would be healed. They had witnessed both ways of healing and knew that Jesus cared enough that He would do something.

When the messenger came back and reported that Jesus wasn't coming and said, "This sickness won't result in death," they were hopeful. Good news! Lazarus wasn't going to die!

But then he did.

What happens to prayer and faith and trust when God doesn't seem to show up when you need Him most?

Jesus finally comes. After the funeral. Lazarus is buried and in the grave and the sisters are still grieving. When Martha gets word that Jesus is on His way, she gets up and goes out to meet Him. I love the faith she greets Him with, "Lord, if you had been here, my brother would not have died. But even now I know that whatever you ask of God, God will give You" (verses 21, 22) When you first read her response, it's easy to think she believes that Jesus could raise Lazarus from the dead. After all, He had raised other people from the dead. But this time was different. Lazarus had been dead four days. The belief was that, after three days, a person's spirit left the area and there was no hope of resurrection. So Jesus comes when all hope is gone. Plus, when Jesus tells the men to roll back the stone, Martha has no expectation or clue what Jesus is about to do. She thinks He just wants to grieve Lazarus. When John writes the story, he mentions that it is *Martha* who says, "Jesus, I don't think you want to do that. It's going to smell pretty bad."

So when she says, "But even now, I believe," she's saying, "But even now that one of the worst possible things has happened and You didn't show up or do anything, I still trust You and believe You are God." In fact, she proclaims that she believes that He is "the Christ, the Son of God, who is to come into the world" (verse 27).[1] She persistently believes Jesus is God and that He loves her and wants what is best for her. She trusts Him despite appearances and feelings.

And Jesus responds with one of His greatest miracles. He saves it for a couple of His best friends. He raises Lazarus from the dead. This story brings me courage. It reminds me that when things don't look like I want them to in response to prayer, that maybe, just maybe, God has something more. That He is going to reveal Himself in ways that I haven't experienced yet. I just need to keep persistently praying and trusting, patiently waiting and watching for what He's doing. He will show up. I need to believe that He loves me and that He *is* hearing me and responding. When Jesus told one father that he just needed to believe, the father replied, "I believe; help my unbelief" (Mark 9:24). It's a prayer each of us can pray, too, in those moments when our belief is intermingled with doubt and fear and when it takes a lot of faith and trust to keep believing because it sure doesn't look like anything is happening.

God loves us. He promises to answer. He promised Paul that His grace was sufficient to keep Paul going despite the thorn in his side. And He promises us the same thing. His grace is sufficient. We need to just keep believing. Sometimes it helps me to pray "believing" prayers, such as, "Lord, I believe that You are working out the answer to this prayer request." "God, I believe that You love this person and that You will move heaven and earth to draw her to You—that You don't want anyone to be lost, not even this person."

Persistent prayers. It's hard. I know. Some of the prayers that still don't look answered are the ones that I have prayed for the longest and want the most. But I keep praying. And I keep reminding myself that He promises to answer. That He does hear. And that He can always be trusted.

What about you?

Are there prayers that you keep praying but are beginning to wonder if God is answering? Or if He even hears?

The enemy will attempt to persuade you to believe that God isn't answering. That He doesn't care. Or he will tempt you to believe that God isn't answering because you're not praying "good enough" or that you yourself aren't "good enough." That if you just got your act together, or if you were a better Christian, God might answer. Don't believe him. He will do anything to cause you to distrust God or give up on prayer. He knows what happens as a result of prayer. And he definitely doesn't want to see you make an impact through prayer. Keep praying. Keep reminding yourself of the truth—what God says about prayer and about you in His Word.

Look for ways that God may be slowly answering your prayers—little movements in the right direction. Ask Him to give you a glimpse of how He's answering. Ask Him to help you believe that He is answering.

Thank Him for the ways He is answering—even if you can't see them. Thank Him for the ways He loves you and loves the person for whom you are praying. Thank Him that you can trust Him to work out every situation for your good (Romans 8:28).

Then just look for Him. He may not answer in the way you are hoping He will, but He will always give you more of Him—a deeper understanding of His love and faithfulness, a peace that you can't explain to anyone else, strength or courage that you know isn't typical for you.

Persistent Prayers

Pray prayers of belief. Pray Scripture promises back to God. If you feel like you don't know what verses to pray, pick up a Bible-promise book. Scriptures are listed in chapters by topic, enabling you to find promises that help meet your specific situation or need.

Then just keep praying. He is answering. And He will do mighty things as a result of your prayers.

---

1. Read the whole story in John 11:1–44.

Chapter 7

Impacting Prayers

Hannah's prayers came from a deeply hurting heart. Her story is found in 1 Samuel beginning in chapter one. The verses introducing her are short and matter of fact, but a deeper look shows a story of heartbreaking pain.

Hannah is married to Elkanah. But she isn't the only one married to him. Elkanah has two wives. Because Hannah was listed first, we can assume she was the first wife. "And he had two wives: the name of one was Hannah, and the name of the other Peninnah" (1 Samuel 1:2a). The description of each wife also gives us a clue that Elkanah married Hannah first and why he took a second wife. "Penninah had children, but Hannah had no children" (verse 2b).

Hannah has no children. In a time and culture where a woman's value was found in her ability to bear her husband sons, Hannah is barren. There was no way for them to know that before they married. After the wedding, they must have eagerly anticipated the day when Hannah would be with child. But months passed and nothing happened. Months turned into years—still no children. This alone had to be heartbreaking. Hannah longs to be a mom, to hold a child of her own. Imagine her going to the market and seeing other women with their rounded bellies slightly visible underneath their robes and watching young moms with their little ones as she walked through the village.

As a woman, she may have felt like a failure, like it was her fault in some way. It would have hurt her to see Elkanah attempt to hide his disappointment month after month. She so wanted to give him the son he longed for.

But there was more to it. Everyone in her village is talking about her. She can see them whispering and looking at her disapprovingly as she passes. People would have assumed that God was cursing her. They believed that when good things happened to you, God was blessing you. But when bad things happened, God was cursing you. And God didn't curse you for no reason; you had to have done something wrong—something very wrong. Her friends may have slowly stopped being friendly. Who wants to be friends with a sinner? Someone who God doesn't even like?

The enemy would have used all of this to constantly discourage Hannah, reminding her over and over that she was a failure. She couldn't do the one thing that was most important for a wife to do. And, he would have told her that God didn't love her. That she was so bad that God had given up on her. She probably battled feelings of hopelessness and worthlessness every single day.

And then there was Peninnah—the other woman.

When did Elkanah decide it was time to bring another woman into the marriage? A woman who could bear him the much-longed-for sons? How many years of pain and sorrow passed before he chose to find a second wife? It was culturally acceptable. Having a son to carry on the family name was super important.

I can't imagine what it was like for Hannah the night Elkanah brought Peninnah home. For her to know that, in the other room, her husband now slept with a (probably) younger wife. While he may have done all he could to assure her that he loved her and that Peninnah was only there to provide children, she felt replaced. She was sharing her husband with another woman. And then when Peninnah's body began changing as a pregnancy became evident, the pain must have pierced Hannah— knowing that another woman carried her husband's child. Something she had not been able to do. And Peninnah is able to do it over and over. She gives Elkanah many sons and daughters (verse 4).

But Peninnah's life is hard too. She is the second wife—the second choice. And her role in the family is very clear. She is there to bear children. Her husband does not love her. She is the means to an end for him. He uses her but loves Hannah. And she is reminded of this every day but especially when they go to the yearly sacrifice in Shiloh. There, when it is time for the offering, Elkanah gives Peninnah and her sons and daughters their portions, but he gives Hannah a double portion, "for he loved Hannah" (verse 5). And everyone sees. Peninnah feels the shame. She feels invisible. A nobody. No matter how hard she tries or how many children she bears, she cannot gain the one thing she wants: to be loved by her husband.

Peninnah channels her hurt and anger and shame into hurting Hannah. "And her rival [Peninnah] also provoked her severely, to make her miserable, because the LORD had closed her womb" (verse 6). Peninnah purposefully and harshly taunts Hannah about her barrenness. She wants Hannah to hurt the way she does. Hannah has what she wants—the love of their husband. And she knows she has what Hannah wants—children. Hurt people hurt other people, and Peninnah hurts Hannah to the point that Hannah is so upset she can't eat. That's huge. Many women run to food for comfort when we're hurting. We are really in pain when we hurt so badly we can't even eat. That's where Hannah was. And the Bible tells us that this happened every year. "Year by year" (verse 7), it was a constant, relentless battle. And it drove Hannah to prayer.

First, Hannah fasts. "She wept and did not eat" (verse 7). When we want to commit to prayer in a deeper way than our typical daily prayers, fasting helps us take that step. When the disciples asked Jesus why they hadn't been able to heal the son a father had brought to them while Jesus was up on the mountain, he told them, "This kind does not go out except by prayer and fasting" (Matthew 17:21). The Greek word for "fasting" used here is *nesteia* and means "self-denial." Fasting was a discipline that demonstrated a deep commitment.

Now, when many of us think about fasting, we think that it means we just stop eating. I know that's what I always thought. So as a young Christian, I committed to fasting one day a week, and it basically meant that one day a week, I didn't eat anything. I used mealtimes as an opportunity to get more done. But fasting is more than just giving up food. It's a commitment to prayer. When we fast, it's a commitment to pray more—so instead of eating, use that time to pray and not just to do something else. And you can choose different ways of fasting. You may want to fast for a day from food. Then during the times you would normally eat, spend that time praying. Or you can decide to fast from something in particular. I often fast from chocolate. So every time I want a piece of chocolate or something chocolate, instead of indulging, I pray. You just have to choose something that you enjoy eating (or drinking). For me to fast from brussels sprouts would be pointless. I rarely, if ever, eat them, so I would rarely, if ever, be reminded to pray for whatever I was fasting and praying about.

But it doesn't have to be a fast from food. I've fasted from reading anything other than the Bible, watching TV, and listening to the radio in the car. And I've fasted from specific habits. (I like to daydream. So once

I fasted from daydreaming. Every time I found myself wanting to drift off into my imagination, I prayed for a young woman in a small group I was teaching. She was involved in an abusive relationship, and it was impacting her other relationships—especially her relationship with God. I fasted for months. She eventually ended the relationship. And when she later met and married a man at her church, she asked me to be a bridesmaid!) I know people who have fasted from social media. Others have fasted but chosen to eat lightly during their fast instead of skipping food altogether. The important thing isn't what you choose to fast from but that you use your fast to remind you to pray more.

But here's a warning: Fasting isn't a guarantee that God will answer your prayers the way you want. It's not about convincing God to respond your way or to respond at all. Remember that God *is* responding—even when you can't see it. It's about deepening our own commitment and relying more on God. I'll admit, I have fasted for a lot of different people and situations, but most have not turned out the way I wanted—at least not right away. But every time of fasting has changed me, helping me know God more intimately and causing me to depend on Him and look to Him more often.

Hannah was totally dependent on God. She couldn't fix it. She couldn't make a baby happen on her own. She desperately needed God. And she told Him so. "And she was in bitterness of soul, and prayed to the Lord and wept in anguish" (1 Samuel 1:10). She laid out her heart. Honestly. I love that! Too often I think we believe that we need to pray beautiful "church" prayers. Yet as I read Hannah's prayers and those of David in the Psalms, I see examples of people praying honest, messy prayers. They weren't pretty and eloquent. They were heartfelt. Hannah was heartbroken. Why did God close her womb? Why did God allow Peninnah to have so many babies but not give Hannah even one? As she prayed she wept—heart-wrenching sobs. She's a mess and she doesn't care. She needs God.

She wants a son desperately, but notice what she does next. "O Lord of hosts, if You will indeed look on the affliction of Your maidservant and remember me, and not forget your maidservant, but will give your maidservant a male child, then I will give him to the Lord all the days of his life" (verse 11). *The Message* Bible says she would give him "completely" and "unreservedly." She prays specifically for what she wants—a *male* child— and then surrenders him—her hopes and dreams—to God. A tough prayer. I want this, but if You give it to me, I'm giving it right back to You. It's Yours. Do with it what You desire. She commits her son—should God say *yes*—to Him *all the days of his life*. She will pray for him, love him, and trust God to do whatever He desires to do in and through this longed-for son.

Commitment is hard sometimes. We want to hold on tight. After all those years and heartbreak, to finally have a son? I wouldn't want to let him out of my sight. But she committed him to God. This shows trust. She trusted God with her hopes and dreams.

While she's praying, the priest sees her praying. It's been a very long time since Eli has seen someone truly connecting with God in a real and honest way. People aren't walking closely with God. And God isn't walking closely with His people as a result. He won't force Himself on them. Eli's own sons, Hophni and Phinehas, are the priests at Shiloh, and they don't know God (1 Samuel 2:12). They don't walk with Him. They don't do what He's called them to do. They won't accept the sacrifices from people the way God commanded—they want the offerings the way they'll taste best to them. And they're sleeping with the women who come to the tabernacle (church). As a result of the priests not knowing or walking with God, people weren't learning about or hearing from God (1 Samuel 3:1). No one was listening. And so Eli doesn't think Hannah is actually praying—he assumes she's drunk and reprimands her for it.

She explains. She tells him that she has "poured out [her] soul before the LORD" (1 Samuel 1:15). She's given everything in her heart and mind to God. The word used for "pour" means "to empty." She has emptied her heart of all the bitterness, the anguish, the hurt. She didn't pour something else into her heart to try to cover up her pain or numb it. She poured out her pain and asked God to fill the ache.

Eli must have been a little surprised to find someone truly seeking God. He tells her, "Go in peace, and the

God of Israel grant your petition which you have asked Him" (verse 17). I think he lifts his own prayers for her and her desires. He instills hope that God will answer.

Here's the cool thing: Hannah listens to Eli and believes. Really believes. She has poured out her heart to God and believes that God will answer. "So the woman went her way and ate, and her face was no longer sad" (verse 18). That's convicting to me. I have to admit there are a lot of times when I pray and pour out my heart, but after giving it to God, I take it back. I keep worrying about it, or hurting over it, or thinking about it. I don't just give it to Him and trust that He's going to respond and step out with peace and joy. *Her face was no longer sad.* She tells herself that God is going to answer, and she waits expectantly, peacefully, joyfully.

We don't know how long she waits. The Bible just says "in the process of time" (verse 20) Hannah conceives and gives birth to a son. She names him Samuel, meaning "Heard by God." As she feels the first stirrings within her abdomen, she knows. God heard her prayers. God is answering her prayers.

As she takes Samuel to Eli and commits him to God, she rejoices and praises God (1 Samuel 2:1–10). It's a reminder that when God answers, we need to thank Him. Remember what He's done. That He's done it. That He loves us. Hears us. It's not because God needs us to say thank you to stoke His ego. It's because of what it speaks into our hearts—that God is a God who is uniquely and daily interested in and involved in our lives.

But Hannah's prayer does more than just bring her that longed for son (and later three more sons and two daughters). Her prayers change the world—they impact the lives of her entire nation.

Remember that God's people were far from Him. They weren't worshiping Him or listening to Him. And because He's a God who doesn't force Himself on people, He was silent. Waiting. Pursuing. Looking for a way to get their attention and cause them to return to Him. He does that through Hannah's prayers. While Samuel is living at the tabernacle and helping Eli, God calls to him. Samuel responds and listens. God calls Samuel to be a prophet and lead His people back to Him. "Then the LORD appeared again in Shiloh. For the LORD revealed Himself to Samuel" (1 Samuel 3:21).

The Lord appears again, speaks again, and leads His people again through Samuel. The boy grew into a man who trusted God and served Him faithfully—all because of the faithful prayers of one woman, who then disappeared from the Bible record. Yet her prayers changed the direction of her people.

What about you?

I want to pray like that. Impacting prayers. Prayers that make a real difference in the world. So what are our takeaways from Hannah's example? How can we pray in a way that changes things?

First, pray honestly. Don't try to "look good" in front of God. He already knows all about you. He knows your bitterness, shame, anger, doubt, etc. He knows your heart—better than you do. Yet He waits for you to completely surrender to Him. Don't worry about praying the right way or the right words. Just pray. Talk to God like you're talking to a friend.

Then surrender completely. Hannah wanted a son, but she told God she would completely surrender Samuel to Him. And she did. I don't know about you, but since Eli hadn't done a great job parenting his own kids, I would not have entrusted my much-longed-for son to him. But really, Hannah wasn't trusting Eli. She was trusting God. She wanted Samuel, but she wanted God more. And she knew she could trust Him. Completely surrender your hopes and dreams to Him. Give God your life and heart unreservedly and trust that He will use you in powerful ways—whether you're aware of it or not.

When it's super important or super hard, fast and pray. I often pray about how to fast. What would God like me to surrender to Him? Then every time I would want to do that or eat that or drink that or check that social media, I would pray instead. I always try to choose something that will truly drive me to pray more. So I want it to be something that's a part of my daily life and, hopefully, scattered throughout my day. Thus I often fast from something I "run to" for comfort. Like chocolate. Or something mindless, like listening to the radio in the car. Instead, I use that alone time to pray. It keeps me focused. And every time I do it, I am encouraged during that time of prayer.

Expect God to answer. Don't keep worrying about it.

Don't keep agonizing. Remind yourself that you've given it to God and that He is answering. It might be helpful to change your prayers, and instead of continuing to ask and cry out to God; thank Him for what He is doing, even if you can't see what He's doing. "God, thank You for the ways You are moving in my friend's life. I know You love them and want so much more than I do for them. You will move heaven and earth for them. Thank You for Your power and strength in their life. I praise You for the ways You are already answering my prayers." Again, this isn't to remind God or convince Him, it's to remind you that God is responding.

And after you experience God's answer, praise Him. Take the time to thank Him. To recount how He has responded and how it has changed you.

What about when you never see the hoped for answer?

A number of years ago, I fasted and prayed for a friend I love. Her marriage was falling apart and she wanted desperately to not only stay married, but for the two of them to truly love each other and be completely committed to each other. I prayed and prayed. Yet their marriage ended. And he quickly remarried someone else. It was heartbreaking for my friend. How do you thank God for that?

Yet I saw God work.

My friend became even more dependent on God. She prayed. She cried. She hurt. But I also saw her grow and blossom into an even more beautiful woman than she was before. She allowed God to work in her life in a deeper way. And slowly He began using her in powerful ways to walk beside other women who were going through divorce. She has an amazing ministry today and is able to speak to the pain that so many women experience—through divorce and through not feeling loved like they long to be loved. And so I praise Him. He didn't force her husband to stay and work things out, though I believe God attempted to draw her husband more deeply to Himself and to his wife. But He answered my prayers on behalf of her and did incredible things for her despite her husband choosing to leave. It still hurts. She still wishes that things had turned out differently and grieves for what could have been, but she loves and knows God in ways that she didn't before. He always gives a deeper experience of Himself.

When you can't see the answers you are looking for, keep trusting God. Believe that He is at work. He is growing you and those you love. He is persistently pursuing and will give you peace and courage no matter what.

God will use your prayers to impact the world, at least your corner of it. Trust Him. Believe it.

Chapter 8

My Prayer for You

*I*t seems like a lifetime ago that I was that little girl just discovering a God who loved me and praying simple prayers of faith. It's amazing how much He has done in my life since then. The places He's taken me. The opportunities He's given me. My mom was just saying yesterday that if anyone had told her back then what I'd be doing now, she would never have believed it.

But, that's what God does—He transforms our lives.

I tell my sons, "God loves you more than I do, and it's hard to believe that anyone can love you more than I do. He has an adventure planned for you, and you are not going to want to miss it."

I think they know it's true. They've seen the adventures God has taken me on—from that shy little girl in the back row to a woman who travels the country speaking to groups about God, His love, and His longing for them. They see how He uses me, allowing my words—written and spoken—to impact others. I know it's not me. I know it's all Him. And I am amazed.

But yes, there are days when I struggle. Battle. Feel

like giving up. I worry way too much about my weight. I want so very much to make a difference in the world, but many days I feel like I'm not accomplishing anything. And I'm often tempted to feel like I'm such a mess there's no way God can ever use me. Of course, He loves proving that's not true. Reminding me that it's not about me and who I am or what I do. It's all about Him and who He is and what He's done.

So even in those discouraging moments, I keep praying. I tell Him my struggles, doubts, and battles honestly. And I praise Him and thank Him for His love and faithfulness and persistent patience with me.

I love Him so very much! He has changed my life. He has changed me.

And He'll do it for you.

I wish that you and I could sit together here in this coffee shop where I'm finishing this book. Enjoy a hot beverage together. I would love to have a real face-to-face conversation about this God who is absolutely crazy about you. I hope these pages have felt like a conversation. I have written honestly from my heart. (And I'll try not to worry too much that you're just thinking, *Thank goodness I'm not as messy as she is!*)

But I want you to know that I am praying for you. I've been praying since before I began writing this and will continue to pray—for these words and for those who will read them. That's you. So when you begin wondering who in the world is praying for you, it's me. I trust that God knows you, knows your name, and knows what you need to hear.

My Prayer for You

And I trust Him to speak His love into your thoughts, give you hope that it's possible, and draw you deep.

I believe one day we will meet. See there is a day coming soon when Jesus is coming back for us. He's promised (John 14:1–3). When He does, He will take us to be with Him in heaven. "For the Lord Himself will descend from heaven with a shout, with the voice of an archangel, and with the trumpet of God. And the dead in Christ will rise first. Then we who are alive and remain shall be caught up together with them in the clouds to meet the Lord in the air. And thus we shall always be with the Lord. Therefore comfort one another with these words" (1 Thessalonians 4:16–18). We will spend eternity with God, learning more about Him and constantly being amazed by His love. We'll get a chance to meet then and share our stories of how He led us and loved us. Until then, I pray you will have the courage to believe that God loves you—yes, you.

Trust Him. Grow deeply. Serve uniquely. Fight the battle. Pray for others. Know that you are forgiven, accepted, chosen, and delighted in.

My prayer for you:

Gracious Heavenly Father,

How I love you! And I know that you are deeply, head over heels in love with the woman who holds this book and is reading these words. The woman who wants to believe that it's true—that You *love* her. *Even if she doesn't have it all together, even when she's not sure that she likes herself; Father God, please, speak Your love to her. Let her hear*

Teach Us to Pray

Your voice above the roar of the world and media and the messages that the enemy has planted in her heart.

Open up Your Word to her as she reads and studies it. Speak to her personally and uniquely—it always amazes me how Your Word can do that. Lead her to promises that she needs to hear. Give her the courage to begin believing them, allowing them to permeate her thoughts and heart.

Father, show her the next step. Show her how You desire to use her to impact the world around her. Help her see (and believe) the gifts and talents You've given her. Help her to trust that You do have a plan for her life (Jeremiah 29:11)—a good plan that will bring her hope. Give her a glimpse of how You are using her.

God, there are people whom she loves who are struggling. Who may not know and trust You. As she lifts them to You in prayer, give her the courage to believe that no matter what it looks like in this moment, You are working. You are hearing and answering. And You will do everything it takes to prepare them for eternity. You will patiently and persistently pursue them, just as You have her.

Oh God, like Paul, I pray that out of Your glorious riches You will strengthen her with power through Your Spirit, so that Christ may dwell in her heart through faith and that she, being rooted and established in love, will have the power to understand how wide, how long, how high, and how deep Your love is, and to know this love that surpasses knowledge—that she may be filled to the measure of all the fullness of You (Ephesians 3:16–19, author's translation).

In Jesus' name, amen.

Prayer Requests

---

*B*efore they call I will answer; and while they are
still speaking I will hear. Isaiah 65:24, NIV

Answered Prayer

I shall give thanks to You, for You have answered
me, And You have become my salvation.
Psalm 118:21, NASB

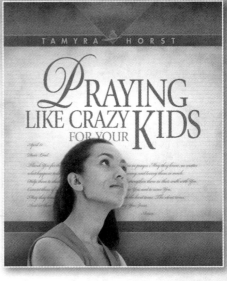

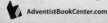
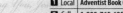

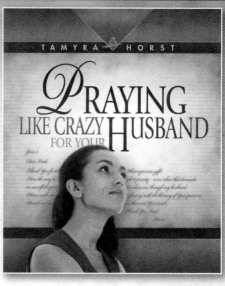

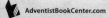

Offering **God's good news** for a better life
today and for eternity